JAMESTOWN EDUCATION

World History Ink

Uprising in Soweto

The McGraw-Hill Companies

Send all inquiries to:

Uprising in Soweto

Racial tension had been growing in South Africa for many years. In the early 1900s, the white government rulers, known as the Boers, allowed very little freedom for blacks and other people of color. The Boers kept firm government control over the region by creating laws that restricted people's lives. Nonwhite persons were not allowed to vote, hold a position in the government, or even receive a good education. As a result, life in South Africa was difficult for anyone who was not white.

In 1948 the government passed apartheid laws. Apartheid means "apart from" or "separate." People were put into a category, or group, based on their race. There were three major categories—white, black, and mixed race. Blacks were no longer accepted as citizens of South Africa. Outside of the towns and cities, areas called townships were set up. Nonwhites were forced to move to the townships, where living conditions were very poor.

Tensions grew in 1974 when a language law was introduced in South African schools. Teachers were required to teach some classes in Afrikaans, the language of the white ruling class. Very few black students could speak or understand Afrikaans. Students' grades in these classes quickly fell.

During this time, a political movement was growing at black colleges and meeting houses. Some teachers encouraged students to demand equal rights and protest unfair laws. On June 16, 1976, in Soweto, a township near Johannesburg, about twenty thousand students walked out of schools in protest against the school language law. Their action served as a call for leadership in the struggle for civil rights.

This is a story of the uprising that changed the course of freedom in South Africa.

OUTSIDE JOHANNESBURG, SOUTH AFRICA
WEDNESDAY, JUNE 9, 1976
AFRIKAANS ENGLISH
WE'RE ALREADY LATE FOR CLASS, SAMORA. ARE YOU SURE THIS IS A SHORTCUT?
THE SOUTH WESTERN TOWNSHIPS, KNOWN TO THE LOCALS AS "SOWETO"
I THINK SO ... IF WE STAY ON THIS STREET AND TURN AT THE NEXT LEFT, WE SHOULD BE AT THE SCHOOL BEFORE THE BELL RINGS.
WELL, I THINK THIS IS THE LONG WAY AROUND.
AFRIKAANS ENGLISH
STOP WORRYING, MIRIAM. EVEN IF WE ARE LATE, NO ONE IS GOING TO NOTICE.
SO YOU THINK THAT IF WE JUST STOP CARING ABOUT OUR EDUCATION, THEY WILL TOO?

THAT KIND OF ATTITUDE IS PART OF THE PROBLEM — STUDENTS HAVE GOT TO —
HEY! HOLD UP A SECOND...
AFRIKAANS ENGLISH

... ISN'T THAT YOUR LITTLE BROTHER?

SIPHO! WHERE ARE YOUR BOOKS?
AND WHY AREN'T YOU IN YOUR SCHOOL UNIFORM?

I STOPPED GOING WEEKS AGO.
YOU WHAT?
WHY SHOULD I? I'M GOING TO END UP STUCK HERE IN SOWETO ANYWAY — SCHOOL OR NOT.

BESIDES, TRYING TO LEARN LESSONS IN AFRIKAANS IS A WASTE OF TIME. I DON'T UNDERSTAND HALF OF WHAT THE TEACHER IS SAYING!
WHY DID THEY MAKE US START TALKING IN THAT DUMB LANGUAGE ANYWAY?
NOTHING IS EVER GOING TO CHANGE IF YOU JUST GIVE UP, SIPHO.

COME ON, WE'RE ALREADY LATE AS IT IS. AND DON'T GET TOO WORKED UP ABOUT LEARNING AFRIKAANS.

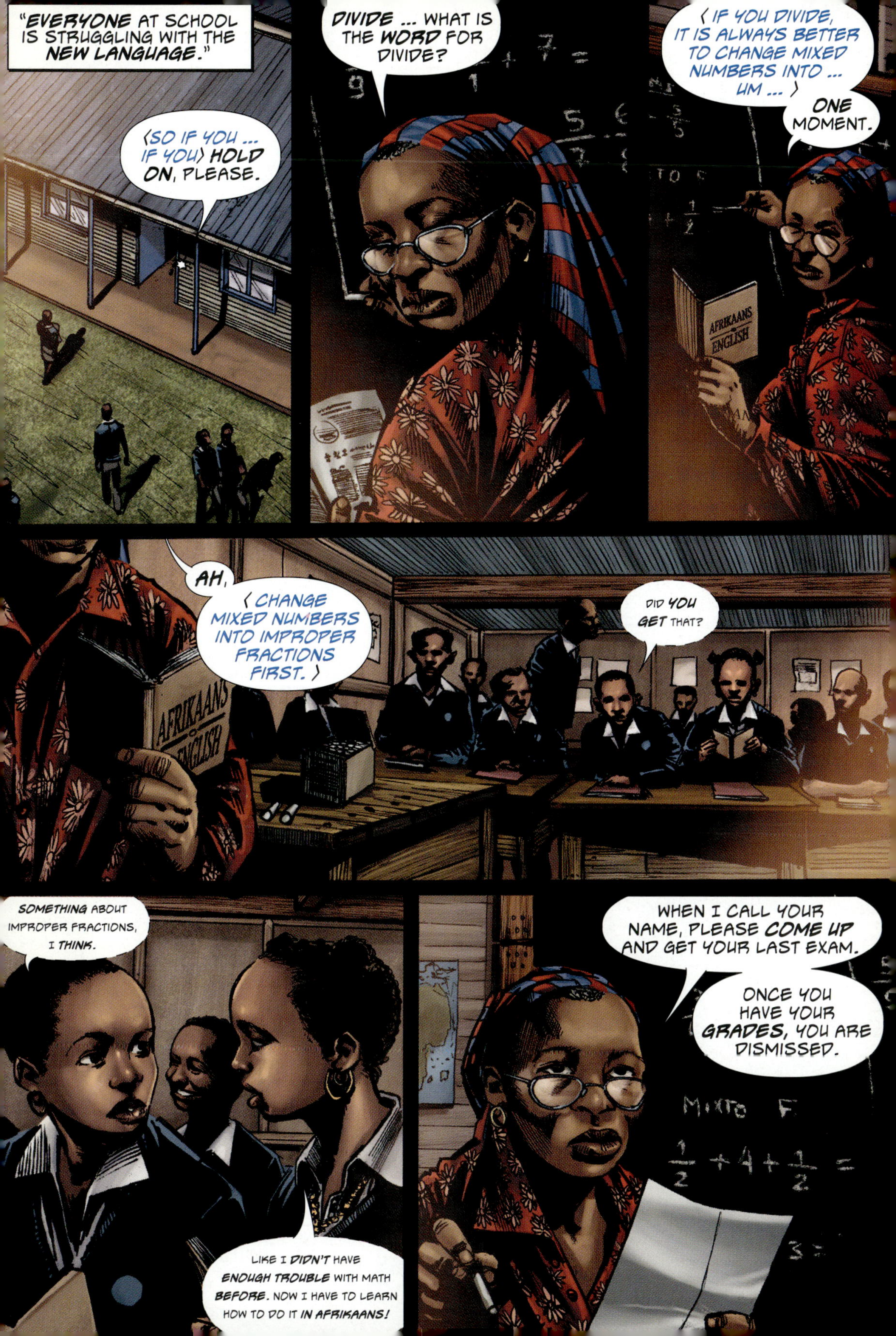

"***EVERYONE*** AT SCHOOL IS STRUGGLING WITH THE ***NEW LANGUAGE.***"

⟨SO IF YOU ... IF YOU⟩ **HOLD ON**, PLEASE.

DIVIDE ... WHAT IS THE ***WORD*** FOR DIVIDE?

⟨ IF YOU DIVIDE, IT IS ALWAYS BETTER TO CHANGE MIXED NUMBERS INTO ... UM ... ⟩

ONE MOMENT.

AFRIKAANS ENGLISH

AH,

⟨ CHANGE MIXED NUMBERS INTO IMPROPER FRACTIONS FIRST. ⟩

AFRIKAANS ENGLISH

DID ***YOU GET*** THAT?

HOW DID YOU DO?
AWFUL.
UGH! YOU AREN'T KIDDING. I'M USED TO DOING POORLY ON TESTS, BUT YOU'RE A MATH WHIZ!
KWAME, HOW CAN I KEEP UP WHEN I CAN'T UNDERSTAND HALF OF WHAT IS BEING TAUGHT ANYMORE?
EVEN MRS. LUKIMBI HAS TO USE A DICTIONARY, AND SHE'S THE SMARTEST WOMAN I KNOW!
MAYBE SIPHO IS RIGHT. WHAT IS THE POINT IN TRYING SO HARD WHEN THE GOVERNMENT IS DETERMINED TO SEE US FAIL?
AFRIKAANS IS ONLY THE LATEST OBSTACLE. DON'T LET IT HOLD YOU BACK, MIRIAM.
I KNOW IT SHOULDN'T, BUT JUST LOOK AT THE CONDITION OF THIS PLACE.
THERE'S NO MONEY FOR NEW BOOKS, WE DON'T HAVE ENOUGH TEACHERS, AND NOW WE HAVE TO TRY TO GET AN EDUCATION IN A LANGUAGE NONE OF US UNDERSTAND.
COME ON, MIRIAM. YOU KNOW IF YOU FAIL, YOU CAN'T BLAME ANYONE BUT YOURSELF.
YOU'RE RIGHT. BUT I'LL TELL YOU THIS —

"— SPEAKING AFRIKAANS ISN'T GOING TO HELP ANY OF US GET OUT OF SOWETO AND AHEAD IN THE WORLD."
ARE YOU GOING TO TELL MOM AND DAD I WAS SKIPPING SCHOOL?
NO. NOT UNLESS YOU DO IT AGAIN.
I WON'T.
GOOD.
LISTEN, I KNOW HOW HARD IT IS. PLEASE PROMISE ME THAT IF YOU EVER GET FRUSTRATED, YOU WILL COME AND TALK TO ME FIRST.
I PROMISE.
MOM. DAD. WE'RE HERE TO HELP.
WHAT ARE WE GOING TO DO? WE CAN'T ORDER ENOUGH GOODS TO FILL OUR SHELVES.

YOU KNOW THE LAWS AS WELL AS I DO. STORES CAN SELL ONLY WHAT THE GOVERNMENT SAYS THE PEOPLE NEED.
IN OTHER WORDS, 'CARRY ONLY THE GOODS WE SAY YOU CAN STOCK.'
THERE'S NO WAY WE CAN SUCCEED IF WE'RE HELD BACK LIKE THIS!
REMEMBER WHEN WE USED TO TALK ABOUT OPENING A BIGGER STORE?
HAH! EACH YEAR, THE LAWS RESTRICT US MORE.
OPEN AT THIS HOUR. CLOSE ON THAT DAY. BE QUIET, AND DO AS YOU ARE TOLD.
I THOUGHT THERE WOULD BE MORE OPPORTUNITIES FOR MIRIAM AND SIPHO HERE IN SOWETO THAN IN THE HOMELANDS.
I WAS WRONG.
ONCE THEY GET THEIR EDUCATION, I HOPE THEY RUN AWAY FROM THIS PLACE AND NEVER LOOK BACK.
IF THINGS DON'T GET BETTER, WE WILL HAVE TO MAKE MORE SACRIFICES.

THURSDAY, JUNE 10, 1976
DID YOU HEAR? A NEW TEACHER IS IN CHARGE OF MRS. BARASA'S SOCIAL STUDIES CLASS.
REALLY? I WONDER WHY?
MRS. BARASA'S FATHER IS VERY SICK. I WILL BE TAKING HER PLACE FOR THE REST OF THE SCHOOL YEAR.
MY NAME IS MR. MUFHADI, AND THIS IS MY FIRST TEACHING ASSIGNMENT.
MY RULES FOR BEHAVIOR ARE SIMPLE AND CAN BE SUMMED UP IN ONE WORD: RESPECT. IF YOU RESPECT EACH OTHER AND RESPECT ME, I'LL RESPECT YOU.
ANY QUESTIONS?
YES?
MY QUESTION IS ABOUT AFRIKAANS. WHY AREN'T YOU SPEAKING IT IN THE CLASSROOM?
BECAUSE VERY FEW OF YOU WOULD UNDERSTAND WHAT I WAS SAYING.

CAN HE DO THAT?
WHAT ABOUT THE LAW?
WELL, I'M NOT GOING TO TELL ON HIM, ARE YOU?
NOT ME. I HATE TRYING TO TALK IN AFRIKAANS.
CAN ANYONE TELL ME WHAT THE WORD ON THE BOARD MEANS?
THAT'S AN AFRIKAANS WORD. IT MEANS SEPARATE.
APARTHEID
CORRECT. THIS ONE WORD IS OUR WAY OF LIFE IN SOUTH AFRICA.
"BEFORE 1960, WHITE MEN ALLOWED BLACK AFRICANS TO LIVE AND WORK IN THEIR CITIES."
"WHY?"
"BECAUSE THEY COULD MAKE MORE MONEY FROM OUR LABOR. BECAUSE IT WAS GOOD BUSINESS."
BUT THEN THE GOVERNMENT GOT INVOLVED AND BEGAN TO TAKE AWAY THOSE RIGHTS. GRAND APARTHEID WAS INTRODUCED.
ALL BLACK AFRICANS IN THE CITIES WERE ASSIGNED NEW PLACES TO LIVE, SEPARATE FROM WHITES.
"POLICE ENFORCED LAWS THAT REQUIRED BLACKS TO CARRY 'PASSBOOKS' WITH THEIR FINGERPRINTS, PHOTOS, AND PROOF THAT THEY WERE ALLOWED INTO THE CITIES."
"WITH EACH PASSING YEAR, THE OPPRESSION HAS BECOME WORSE."

"SO, NOW WE HAVE THE AFRIKAANS MEDIUM DECREE OF 1974, WHICH REQUIRES MATHEMATICS AND SOCIAL STUDIES BE TAUGHT IN AFRIKAANS."
"WHICH I WILL BE PLEASED TO DO, ONCE ALL OF YOU HAVE LEARNED THE LANGUAGE WELL ENOUGH TO PROPERLY DO YOUR ASSIGNMENTS. CLASS DISMISSED."
THAT WAS AMAZING! EVERYTHING IS CONNECTED!
SHHHH! NOT SO LOUD.
THAT TEACHER IS GOING TO GET ALL OF US IN TROUBLE. HE'S BREAKING THE LAW, AND WE'RE LETTING HIM!
SAMORA, IT'S A LAW THAT NONE OF US AGREE WITH. BESIDES, HE WAS TALKING ABOUT OUR OWN HISTORY!
MRS. BARASA SAID, "IF YOU WANT TO UNDERSTAND TODAY, YOU HAVE TO SEARCH YESTERDAY."
AFRIKAANS ENGLISH
LISTEN TO YOURSELF! THE WAY YOU ARE GOING ON, YOU SOUND LIKE YOU WANT TO JOIN THE PROTEST MOVEMENT!
WHO KNOWS? MAYBE I WILL!

FRIDAY, JUNE 11, 1976
IF YOU WANT TO MAKE A DIFFERENCE, THEN YOU HAVE TO BE A PART OF THE SOUTH AFRICAN STUDENT MOVEMENT.
THE ONLY WAY WE'RE GOING TO SEE CHANGE IS BY MAKING IT HAPPEN OURSELVES.
YOU CAN HELP SPREAD THE WORD ABOUT THE MOVEMENT HERE AT MORRIS ISAACSON HIGH.
I'M JUST WORRIED ABOUT HOW MY PARENTS WOULD REACT.
HAVE YOU HEARD? THEY FIRED MR. MUFHADI!
SOMEONE TOLD THE HEADMASTER THAT MR. MUFHADI WASN'T SPEAKING AFRIKAANS. THEY TOLD HIM TO START, OR HE WAS OUT.
I DON'T BELIEVE IT! HE WAS THE FIRST TEACHER I'VE HAD AT THIS SCHOOL THAT MADE ME CARE ABOUT HISTORY. THIS ISN'T FAIR.
COUNT ME IN, TSIETSI. IF THEY GOT RID OF A TEACHER LIKE MR. MUFHADI AFTER ONLY A DAY, WHERE IS IT GOING TO STOP FOR THE REST OF US?
ON SUNDAY, WE'LL MEET WITH STUDENTS FROM ALL ACROSS SOWETO.

"SPREAD THE WORD. WE HAVE TO LET PEOPLE KNOW WHAT IS GOING ON IN OUR SCHOOLS."
CHILD, IF YOU KNOW WHAT IS GOOD FOR YOU — FOR ALL OF US — YOU WILL STAY OUT OF POLITICS.
HOW ARE THINGS GOING TO CHANGE IF NO ONE SAYS ANYTHING?
MIRIAM, SPEAKING OUT IS A GOOD WAY TO GET KILLED!
END APARTHEID NOW
"HIS NAME WAS DANIEL, AND HE WAS MY FRIEND."
"WE WERE PROTESTING PEACEFULLY, BUT THAT DIDN'T MATTER."
"ALL IT TOOK WAS ONE FALSE MOVE ..."
"... AND ONE SCARED FINGER ON THE TRIGGER OF A RIFLE."
THIS IS DIFFERENT. ALL WE WANT TO DO IS SPEAK OUT AGAINST AFRIKAANS.
MIRIAM, DON'T YOU UNDERSTAND?
THE DAY ENDED IN VIOLENCE. THE DAY ENDED WITH DANIEL'S DEATH.

"TO PROTEST AFRIKAANS IS TO PROTEST APARTHEID ITSELF."
SUNDAY, JUNE 13, 1976
TO MAKE A DIFFERENCE, ONE PERSON CANNOT STAND ALONE. WE HAVE TO JOIN TOGETHER IF WE ARE GOING TO BE HEARD!
THE USE OF AFRIKAANS IS BUT ONE OF A HUNDRED WAYS WE HAVE BEEN MISTREATED.
HOWEVER, IT IS ALSO WHAT HAS UNITED US!
THEY WILL SEE US WALK OUT OF CLASS AND TRY TO STOP US, BUT WE WILL NOT BE HELD BACK.
JUNE 16 WILL NOT BE A WEDNESDAY — JUNE 16 WILL BE OUR DAY!
WHAT ABOUT OUR PARENTS? CAN WE INVOLVE THEM AS WELL?
GOOD QUESTION, AND THE ANSWER IS NO.
OUR PARENTS ARE OF A GENERATION THAT WILL NOT FIGHT, AND THEY WILL STOP US. WE MUST MAKE A PACT TO KEEP OUR PLANS A SECRET.

"WE WILL LET ONLY THE LEADERS OF THE SOUTH AFRICAN STUDENT MOVEMENT ACROSS THE CITY KNOW ABOUT OUR PLAN."
"ALL OF THEM, IN TURN, WILL SPREAD THE WORD TO OTHER STUDENTS AT THEIR SCHOOLS."
"WE WILL HAVE A PEACEFUL MARCH, BUT NOT ONLY FOR STUDENTS. IT IS ALSO FOR ALL THOSE WHO HAVE BEEN ABUSED AND FORGOTTEN BY APARTHEID."
"THIS DEMONSTRATION IS FOR US ALL."
WE SHALL WALK OUT OF SCHOOL TOGETHER ON WEDNESDAY AND MEET AS ONE

TUESDAY, JUNE 15, 1976

ARE YOU SURE IT IS SAFE HERE, MIRIAM?

YES, MY PARENTS ARE CLEANING THE STORE TONIGHT.

SIPHO'S THERE TOO, SO WE HAVE THE HOUSE TO OURSELVES.

SO WHY ISN'T SAMORA HELPING?

SO TOMORROW WE SET OFF FOR ORLANDO WEST JUNIOR SECONDARY SCHOOL, RIGHT?
RIGHT! AND THEN ONWARD TO ORLANDO STADIUM!
OH! – UM, GOOD EVENING MR. AND MRS. MOHAPI.
YOU'RE EARLY.
AND YOU SHOULD BE IN BED, NOT INVOLVING YOUR LITTLE BROTHER IN THIS BUSINESS.
THIS HAS TO STOP, MIRIAM. WHATEVER YOU HAVE PLANNED, WE MUST END IT TONIGHT.
TATA, YOUNG BLACK AFRICANS CAN CONTINUE TO DO AS WE ARE TOLD ...
GO TO BED!
... OR WE CAN TAKE ACTION. WE MUST IMPROVE OUR SCHOOLS AND EDUCATION SO WE CAN HAVE A LIFE WITH A FUTURE.
WAIT.

PERHAPS YOU ARE RIGHT. MY GENERATION HAS GROWN TO ACCEPT WHAT WE ARE GIVEN.
WE HAVE STOPPED DREAMING OF WHAT LIFE COULD BE.
AND WE HAVE A RIGHT TO BE TAUGHT IN ENGLISH. I DON'T WANT TO KEEP SKIPPING SCHOOL BECAUSE OF AFRIKAANS.
I'M READY TO FIGHT TO MAKE THINGS BETTER – AND I'M NOT THE ONLY ONE.
LISTEN, I WANT YOU BOTH TO UNDERSTAND SOMETHING.
ALL YOUR FATHER AND I HAVE EVER WANTED IS FOR YOU TO SUCCEED IN LIFE AND BE HAPPY.
NOW GO TO BED, BOTH OF YOU. WE'LL DISCUSS THIS FURTHER IN THE MORNING.
SO, WHAT DO WE DO NOW?
WE FOLLOW OUR DAUGHTER'S EXAMPLE AND MAKE A CHOICE.

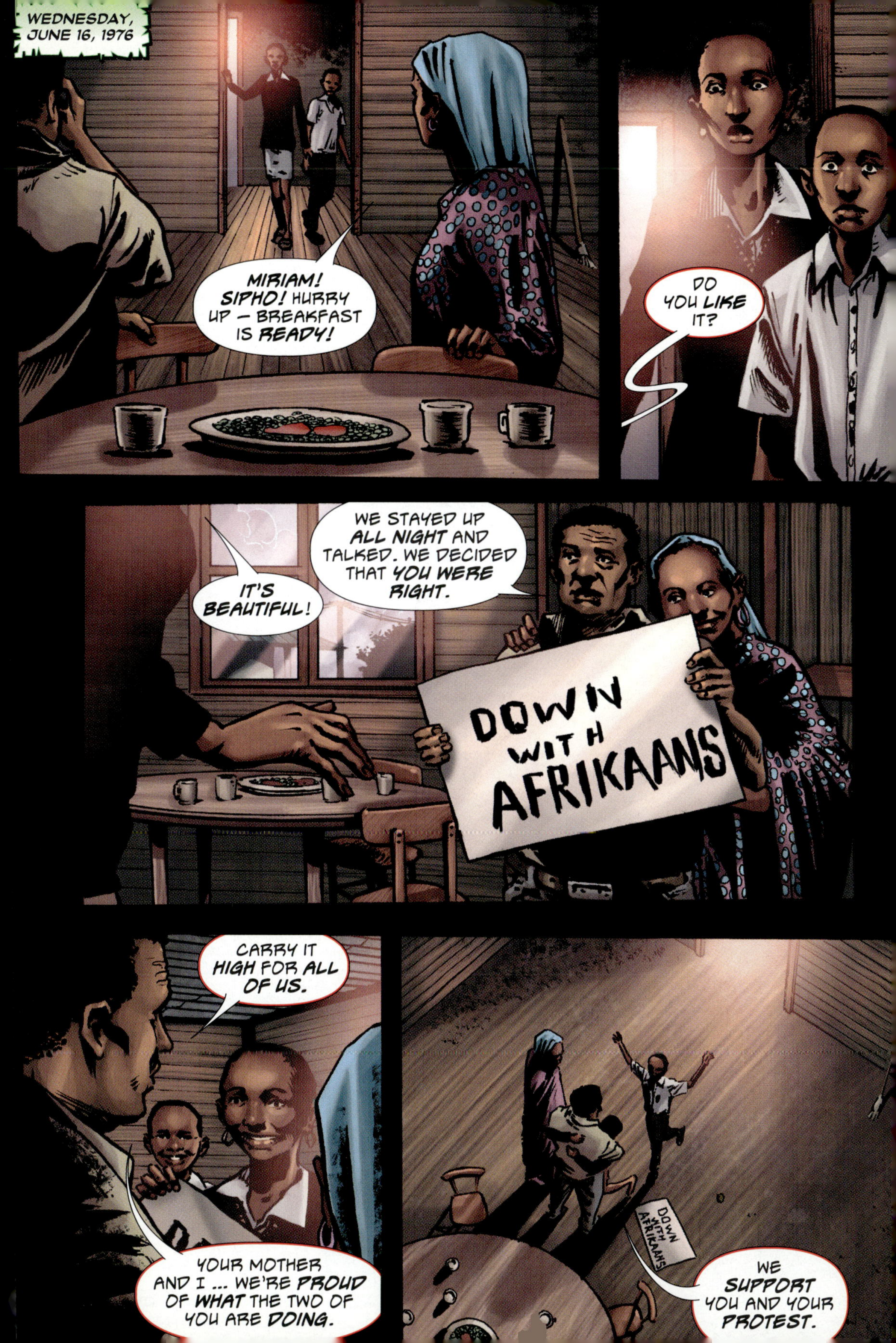

WEDNESDAY, JUNE 16, 1976

MIRIAM! SIPHO! HURRY UP — BREAKFAST IS READY!

DO YOU LIKE IT?

"SO WHEN YOU WALK OUT OF YOUR SCHOOLS TODAY, AND LET YOUR VOICES BE HEARD IN PROTEST OF AFRIKAANS, REMEMBER THIS."
Nkosi, sikelel' iAfrika
Malupakam'upondo lwayo
Yiva imitandazo yetu
Usisikelele.
"REMEMBER THAT WE LOVE YOU AND CHERISH YOU."
DOWN WITH AFRIKAANS
"YOU ARE THE BRAVE ONES MAKING A STATEMENT."
NO TO APARTHE
"YOU ARE THE ONES WHO CAN SEE THE FUTURE AND WHO WILL MAKE A DIFFERENCE."
DOWN WITH AFRIKAANS
NO TO APARTHEID
BY 10:30 A.M., MORE THAN FIVE THOUSAND STUDENTS HAD GATHERED, WITH MORE ARRIVING EVERY MINUTE.
WITNESSES LATER PUT THE TOTAL AT ABOUT TWENTY THOUSAND.
THE POLICE FORMED A HUMAN WALL IN RESPONSE.
THE PROTESTORS WERE MET WITH TEAR GAS, ATTACK DOGS, AND BULLETS.
TWENTY-THREE PEOPLE DIED THAT DAY IN SOWETO, AND HUNDREDS MORE WERE INJURED.
DOWN WITH AFRIKAANS
NO TO APARTHEID
DOWN WITH AFRIKAANS
NO TO APARTHEID
NO TO APARTHEID
THE SOWETO PROTEST WAS THE POLITICAL TURNING POINT IN THE STRUGGLE AGAINST APARTHEID.
SOUTH AFRICA WAS NEVER THE SAME AGAIN.

Some Important People

Teboho "Tsietsi" Mashinini

Tsietsi Mashinini was born in 1957 in Soweto. He attended Morris Isaacson High School and became a powerful speaker on the student debate team. Mashinini gave many speeches about the poor conditions of life for black people. He persuaded his fellow students to march in a nonviolent protest against the Afrikaans language in the schools. On June 16, 1976, thousands of students left school in the morning and marched in protest. Mashinini's hope for a peaceful protest was destroyed when police arrived and started shooting at students. He urged the students to get out of danger and go home. However, Mashinini himself was never able to go home. The government wanted to punish him for helping organize the march. He hid from police for more than two months before leaving South Africa forever. Yet the march did have a positive outcome. The government let schools return to teaching in whatever language worked best for students. Today Mashinini is honored as a hero in the struggle against apartheid.

Amy Biehl

In August 1993, apartheid was finally coming to an end. South Africans were about to have the first election in which all adult citizens would be allowed to vote. Amy Biehl was twenty-six years old and from the United States. She was in South Africa to study the changes taking place and to help people register to vote. One night after work, Biehl drove three other workers home in Guguletu, a black township. A group of young black men saw her and became angry at the sight of a white person. They didn't know who she was or that she had been working to make South Africa a better place. They forced her car to stop, and then they pulled her from the car and killed her. Four young men were convicted of murder and sentenced to eighteen years in prison. Biehl's death shocked the country. Blacks and whites joined together to march in peace rallies. After visiting Guguletu, Amy Biehl's parents announced they would carry on their daughter's work. They set up an organization called the Amy Biehl Foundation, which teaches job skills to black South Africans. The four young men were released from prison after serving only four years. Biehl's parents agreed with this decision to release them. They even hired two of the men to work for the organization that was named after their daughter.

Nelson Mandela

Nelson Mandela joined a political group called the African National Congress (ANC) in the early 1940s. This group took part in nonviolent protests, strikes, and marches. Its goal was to pressure the government to give equal rights to black people. The South Africa government put many ANC members in jail. Mandela decided that nonviolence was not going to change the government. He trained people to fight for their rights with weapons. As a result, Mandela was sentenced to life in prison for planning to overthrow the government. Mandela served twenty-seven years in prison. Then, in 1990, South African president F. W. de Klerk released him. Mandela and the president worked together to end violence and give all South Africans equal rights. The two men shared the Nobel Peace Prize in 1993. One year later, in the country's first democratic election, Mandela was elected as South Africa's first black president.

BLACK SOUTH AFRICA'S

1652

The Dutch East India Company settles the Cape Colony at the southern tip of Africa. Dutch farmers (called Boers) later spread throughout the area and take land from African tribes.

1806

Great Britain takes control of the Cape Colony.

1816–1826

Shaka Zulu becomes leader of the Zulus and helps build the Zulu Empire.

1835–1840

Thousands of Boers leave the Cape Colony and settle on land farther north and east.

1879

The British defeat the Zulus in a six-month war. Eight years later, the British control the Zulus' land.

1910

After several years of fighting, the British and the Boers join together to form the Union of South Africa.

1910–1936

Several laws are passed that limit the rights of blacks to vote, get jobs, own land, and travel with freedom.

1912

The South African Native National Congress is formed to organize Africans in the struggle for civil rights. This political party later becomes the African National Congress (ANC).

1948

The National Party, a strongly pro-white group, wins the election. The government soon passes apartheid laws. These laws classify all South Africans by race, prohibit mixed-race marriages, and force blacks to live in separate areas.

STRUGGLE FOR POWER

1952

"Pass laws" require all blacks to carry "passbooks" for identification. The laws also forbid blacks from living or working in any town without government permission. The ANC begins mass protests.

1960

A large group of blacks in the township of Sharpeville protests against the pass laws. Police gunfire kills sixty-nine protestors. This sparks more protests, and the government answers by making the ANC illegal.

1963

Nelson Mandela, head of the ANC, is jailed and later sentenced to life in prison. Many other protest leaders and critics of the government are jailed.

1976

Police open fire on thousands of students in the black township of Soweto when they protest against an unfair education rule. This sparks more riots across the country. The government brings on more violence. People and governments around the world criticize and boycott South Africa.

1978–1989

The government makes some changes, but most segregation remains, and nonwhites are kept out of power. Worldwide pressure against South Africa increases.

1990

New president F. W. de Klerk ends apartheid laws. Mandela is released from prison after twenty-seven years.

1993–1994

All citizens eighteen and older are given the right to vote. Many social and political rights are guaranteed to all citizens. Mandela is elected president of the new South Africa.

CHARACTER DESCRIPTION

Choose one of the characters from *Uprising in Soweto*. Write the character's name in the center oval of the word web below. In the outer ovals, write words that describe the character. Then use the words in sentences that explain why the word describes the character. Use the lines below the word web to write your sentences.

Example sentence: Miriam is honest, because she keeps her promise to her brother.

1.

2.

3.

4.

5.

6.